Wealthy in the Woods

A call to deeper, richer, and healthier living

Debbie Tuttle

Wealthy in the Woods

Copyright © 2018 Debra A Tuttle
Barefoot Heart Publishing

All rights reserved. No part of this book may be reproduced or transmitted in any form or by any means, electronic or mechanical, including photocopying, recording, or by any information storage and retrieval system, without permission in writing from the publisher. All rights reserved for translation into foreign languages. No liability is assumed with respects to use of the information contained in this volume.

Disclaimer: Information in this book has not been evaluated by the Food and Drug Administration, and is for educational purposes only. It is not intended to diagnose, prescribe, advise, treat, or cure any disease, ailment, injury, infirmity, deformity, pain, or any other condition, physical or mental.

Published by Barefoot Heart Publishing
P.O. Box 68083
Portland, OR 97268-9998
1.503.334.9114

For grandchildren to make memories:
Jenea, Jaren, Jolia, Jude, Jadon, Jenevieve, Jordyn, Loryn,
Zackery, Preston, Kiera, and all to come.

Table of Contents

1: Dear You 7

2: What does Wealthy in the Woods look like? 9

3: The Official Reason 14

4: The Real Reason 17

5: Our Bodies 19

6: Connection to Self 23

7: Walking for Your Life 26

8: Energy of the Land 29

9: Animals: Our Companions 32

10: Love Our Convenience! 35

11: The Network Marketing Tool........................... 38

12: Exploring Further 42

Recommended Books 43

Essential Oils Reference 44

Index and Resources 47

About the Author 49

1: Dear You

My Dear Reader:

Since you have this book in hand, I know some things about you. You are curious and open to learning potentially life-changing ideas. You've worked hard serving others on your chosen path, whether it paid well or not because you believed in the value of what you do.

You may feel your life is too complicated, too busy to enjoy the amazing journey on a miraculous planet full of beauty, strength, variety, spirit, and healing.

You wish your *get-away-from-it-all* daydreams or vacations could be your everyday life, but you also enjoy using your gifts and talents to serve others. A simpler life without time or money stress sounds *sooooo* nice.

Meaningful, passionate work is important, but you would also love to have quiet time to journal, reflect, garden, or paint, balanced with social time for family, friends, and humanitarian service. Maybe you'd like travel, classes, and local events mixed in. Not to mention recreation that excites you, whether that is gallery openings or wind-surfing or gourmet cooking.

You have faced trials and still face challenges, which have given you both scars and sorrows. They've also given you compassion, strength, wisdom, and personal power.

Are you with me?

You appreciate the contentment of life that includes comfy furniture, a fire crackling in the winter, cool breeze in the summer, delicious, wholesome food, and abundant clean water. You appreciate opportunities to see and experience natural wonders of the world.

There's no doubt that getting outdoors re-fuels you personally, and you believe that time in nature is crucial to your physical, mental, emotional, and spiritual well-being. That it can help heal our wounds, strengthen your relationships, and connect you to the point in your life where sharing your gifts (as well as the gifts of the earth) has become important.

The conversations I had with a few like-minded entrepreneurs while gathering thoughts for this book gives me great hope for collaboration. We, as partners across the world, can guide others to appreciate, respect, be healed by, and love nature. We can do this while attracting an income that allows the time and financial freedom to evolve into our highest purposes.

Wealthy in the Woods is an image that works for me, but maybe your dreams are for an oceanfront, a high desert, or a nomadic life. What's common between us is the hunger to live near, act wisely in, and share the natural world.

I look forward to hearing about your dreams and goals and explore ways to lift each other to them. This book is an introduction to abundant natural living; plans for future publications include spotlighting more of us.

Hugs and Blessings,
Debbie

2: What does Wealthy in the Woods look like?

Asking twenty people who are drawn to nature what "wealthy in the woods" looks like will result in twenty different answers. Some picture a log cabin-style mansion on a hill overlooking a lake. Others envision a cozy place of solitude, snuggled up on a comfy couch in front of a fire with a cup of hot cocoa and a good book or movie or friend. What's most important is how they'll feel living there.

Living in the woods is NOT about deprivation, being a hermit (though sometimes a brief period of hermitage sounds fabulous), nor cluttered, dingy living. I'm not suggesting subsistence living or the absence of any enriching activities which bring meaning to our life.

There's no right or wrong vision, but I noticed common themes with those I interviewed.   They are:

Comfort. Physically, whatever activity happens outdoors, it's all about comfort indoors. The furniture, cozy beds, temperature, and color schemes relax us. Emotionally, we're living where we can sink into a restorative place and renew ourselves. Here's the first place the wealth idea comes in. When we have a sufficient income from past and present work, we feel calm knowing our needs are met. In this place of trust, we can focus on our life's highest missions.

Safety. On both practical and emotional levels, we feel safe. Sometimes it's because we're hidden away from the rest of the world, which offers respite from external stresses and pressures. People who visit our space or who live nearby are also safe. You have their backs, and they have yours. Wild animals -- I'm thinking bear here -- cannot get inside our cottages, but since we share space with them, their lives and needs are respected. This safe place allows us the opportunity to explore our deepest selves.

Space. There is space of time and distance from city life, even if we enjoy its hustle and bustle and energy. It's all about balance, right? As an introvert, I like people and look forward to social events, but also need solitude and quiet to recharge. I draw my energy from solitude. Extroverts, who recharge when they're with others, also appreciate quiet to reflect or face deeper issues. And life in the woods can be full of fun, activity, and action, as desired. The vibe of the natural world supports our wellness and satisfaction.

Simplicity. There is less chatter and "stuff" cluttering our lives. Instead, we focus on meaningful conversations with self or others, thoroughly enjoying what we mindfully choose to keep. My vision is to live modestly, not because I can't afford more, but because I prefer quality over quantity and have the means to be discerning. I believe that voluntary simplicity allows us to live more deeply and richly. Developing talents, relationships, and ourselves brings more satisfaction than collecting meaningless items.

Natural beauty. Beauty surrounds and envelops us. Often, water is part of my picture, whether a little creek near my house or a recreational lake for water sports nearby. I love trees and forest ambiance (hence the title of the book), but I also love sandy beaches, palm trees, and tropical climates, especially in the winter. Bamboo forests in Hawaii are as incredible as the evergreen forests of the Pacific Northwest U.S. where I live. As far as a home, I visualize anything from a timber A-frame to a sheltered, stone home to a place spacious enough for family reunions. Regardless of the type of building, it incorporates the beauty of nature and breathtaking views.

Relationships. Healthy, loving, mutually uplifting relationships make life worthwhile. To love and be loved, to develop ourselves and help develop others' gifts and talents bring deep satisfaction to most of us. In nature, nothing is wasted or unwanted. We feel that value in ourselves when we take the time to notice.

There are many senses beyond the five we learn about that can be awakened and filled by connection with nature. Michael J. Cohen, having spent over thirty-five years living mostly outdoors, lists fifty-three. He contends that disconnection is the source of many of our cultures mental and physical health issues. Perhaps we are hungry to be filled in ways that indoor living can't offer.

Wealth. Beyond wealth as money, we can be rich on a multitude of levels. We have an ongoing income that not only meets our physical needs but helps other people in crisis or chronic need. It allows us to create our dream life, support causes we know to be important, and more fully express our best selves. We can feel wealthy in the vast variety and diversity of the earth's life, in what humanity is continually discovering about the universe, and in the opportunities to learn, grow, and reinvent ourselves however we desire.

Wealth in this context is all about abundance.

When I become interested in a new topic, one of my first acts is to hit the library and internet for information and gather resources. Seeing hundreds of books at my fingertips gives me a feeling of incredible wealth, whether those books are on my home's shelves or elsewhere. I know there are treasures of wisdom in every single one.

My definition of wealth is:

- To be involved in networking and educational courses that expose me to new ideas, supportive communities, and amazing people;
- To feel my grandchildren's hugs and kisses;
- To see that our grown children seem to enjoy spending time with us;
- To have my husband's love, support, and backrubs;
- To have a purring friend on my lap in the evening; and
- To use spiritual practices to draw close to God and the realms beyond what we sense physically; and
- To spend lots of time outdoors.

So the simple answer to what Wealthy in the Woods looks like is the means and opportunity to live, work, and play connected to the natural world, with income that easily lets us do whatever will bring us the most comfort, fulfillment, and joy.

I'm not there yet, but my wealthy-in-the-woods life is being formed in vision, plans, and action. I explore and refine my vision further by talking with people whose work includes connection, time, and interacting with the outdoors. My purpose is to inspire our way of being in nature, to offer principles that help us come closer to the vision and to show that it is possible to live exactly as we desire.

3: The Official Reason

Ecopsychology is a science which merges ecology and psychology. If you look up the definition, you'll discover various explanations. The sense I get from people involved in this field is connecting with nature is a powerful and effective way of helping us become whole, aware, and well.

Benefits of living a life connected with nature are being confirmed by study after study. Here's my truth: I don't need the studies to believe it. I experience it.

Still, the research is impressive. Here are a couple of examples:

Richard Louv, the author of *Last Child in the Woods* and *The Nature Principle*, cites numerous studies and shares anecdotes, about the human health connection with nature. He notes that when people connect with nature, they have enhanced brain activity and creativity; lower rates of obesity and depression; and better health, wellness, relationships, and fun.

Psychotherapist Philip Chard, the author of *The Healing Earth*, uses nature in his therapies effectively and extensively. He asserts that the healing and help nature offers comes from immediate experience, not by faith in something unseen.

I am convinced our estrangement from nature has led to poor mental, physical, and spiritual health and that the earth itself as a bit of the universe has a healing energy we can tap into.

I live in the often cloudy, rainy Pacific Northwest of the United States, and, fortunately, subdued light doesn't affect me. There are plenty of indoor activities to enjoy, and rain gear for outdoors. But when I haven't been outside for a while, I experience food cravings, irritability, and lower quality sleep. When I get back outside, not by looking at pictures or through windows, but outside, a deep peace returns to me. And when the sun comes out after months of gray—Wow! People stream outdoors and exude cheerfulness we hadn't realized was missing. For me, outdoor time partners with faith as a principle of power.

When we connect with the energy of plants, trees, water, animals, and the land we sense spirit much greater than ourselves. While humbling us, we also feel our value in that bigger scheme. We knew deep in our bones that we're here on purpose, for a purpose, and we are loved.

I feel healthier and happier when I get some outdoor time every day. But since I can't be in a forest all day to breathe the air and oils released naturally by fir trees, flowers, leaves, and roots, I often use plant essential oils to get the same health benefits as being outside. Putting essential oils on or into our bodies can be one of the most intimate ways we connect with nature as they literally become part of us. I want good things to counteract and replace the harmful substances surrounding us in modern life.

As I write today, a combination of oils to increase motivation and peace are diffusing in my office. You could probably get a lot of information about me from looking at my oil choices (happy face here). My current stresses and concerns show up in the oils I use.

Research and anecdotal evidence show essential oils help us process, release, and resolve emotions while uplifting us. But again, experience gives personal proof of the value. Anywhere. Everywhere.

4: The Real Reason

"If all the beasts were gone, men would die from a great loneliness of spirit, for whatever happens to the beasts also happens to the man. All things are connected."
~ Chief Seattle of the Suquamish Tribe in a letter to President Franklin Pierce

The science reasoning from the last chapter satisfies our reasonable mind, but the more compelling motivation is the personal, positive experience that we cherish.

Currently, I'm reading a book (one of about six I have going) called *Reconnecting with Nature*, and love the science, ideas, and activities described in it. I'm reminded to be outdoors part of every day and to consciously reach out to feel the energy of trees, birds, and land, even if I'm just walking up the street to the mailbox. Being outdoors fills a place in me that no amount of chocolate can (and I do enjoy good chocolate).

Today, after an intense phone call with one of my grown children who is struggling, I took a walk outside before sitting down to write. Doing this brought me back to calm, back to the still pool of truth in the depths of me. I sat on the porch petting one of the outdoor cats after that short walk and invited the *beautifuls* (as I call the local hummingbirds) to say, "Hi," from a nearby tree. One barely flitted by. Within a couple of minutes, there were at least ten chickadees gathered and hopping all over my bare crepe myrtle tree. They danced with me, coming closer, then skittering away, returning closer to peek at me, and then away. Now that I'm in my office looking at the same tree, they are gone. It thrills me when animals, or small children for that matter, respond to the love I send out.

Because they do.

5: Our Bodies

"The first wealth is health." ~ Ralph Waldo Emerson

We have a physical and an energetic or spiritual interface with the world around us. There is no way to avoid the exchange of substances that we're immersed in, simply because we're alive. But we do have some control over the quality of what comes into our bodies. We can work as a community to ensure we have clean water, air, and food supplies in the long run. In the short term, we can choose carefully.

In some my herbal medicine studies, we used a funny metaphor for our bodies: an elongated donut. Imagine that our skin covers the outside of the donut, and our intestinal tract runs along the edge of the donut hole. This means that the lining of the mouth, esophagus, stomach, and intestines are part of our interface with the world. What this lining comes in contact with from a source outside of us (e.g., food, water, medications, and whatever else we consume), has a physical, chemical, and energetic effect on us. The energy, or vibration, can be measured in Megahertz (MHz).

If we want truly to be wealthy, abundant, and fulfilled, being as healthy as possible at the moment is paramount. We aim for holistic health that functions in the present, but we take action for higher levels of health in the future.

Consider air and water quality. While we can filter water and air in our homes, cleaning and purifying them, we are exposed to who-knows-what as soon as we step outside—no matter where we are (although getting away from the concentrated pollutants of cities makes a difference). Plants are great purifiers, adding another reason to get to the woods when possible.

Think about food quality. There are books, whole courses, websites, and careers dedicated to nutrition, although they often offer conflicting information. Sadly, for many of us, it can be difficult to get all the nutrients we need from our food today, no matter how healthy we try to eat. For various reasons, including soil depletion, eating healthy is a challenge.

I recently read that to get the nutrition from one carrot eaten in the 1970s; we have to eat twelve carrots today. Another source suggests for one orange in the seventies, we'd need eight today. That's shocking, right?

My studies and experience have convinced me that plant-based eating habits bring the most benefit to us and the earth. I don't necessarily mean going completely vegetarian, but eating a high percentage of whole plant-based foods. That said, food-based dietary supplements are recommended by many experts to fill in the nutrition gap left by our current food supply.

Even the bath, beauty, and skin care products we use matters. Everything we put on our bodies gets into our bodies, to a greater or lesser degree. That's especially true for the bottom of our feet, which have some of the largest pores in our body. So we can look at ingredients and choose more natural, even beneficial, substances to use.

When I think of my feet and the cleaning products I've used—then walked on barefoot—I actually get scared. Outdoor grunge, indoor chemicals. What have we put on/in our bodies by way of laundry products, floor cleaners, fabrics, and paints?

We're not going to be able to avoid everything that's hard on our bodies, but we can be aware and counter any negative effects where practical.

In my first book, *Seven Secrets of Shining*, I discussed toxic load. From the time we are born and throughout our lives, organisms, radiation, and chemicals that can hurt our bodies and minds bombard us. They can slow functioning and bring painful sensations, reducing our energy and wellness. Digestive, respiratory, and hormone imbalances are some of the issues many of us face that may be related to our toxic load. Threats to our wellness are handled by our amazing bodies supported by what we put on and in them. They're also supported by what we surround ourselves with—the people, things, other life forms, even ideas, and attitudes.

There are two aspects to toxic load. First, what we already have in our bodies just by living, from drinking water and breathing air, from past gut-imbalance substances to chemical-laden cosmetics. Many of them aren't excreted or metabolized, so our body quarantines them as best as they can to minimize internal damage-- meaning they are stored in various tissues, mainly adipose or fat tissue. We want to help our bodies get rid of them. Periodic detoxing sessions by diet, massage, and other practices, including specific essential oils, can be effective.

Second, what we are putting into our bodies in our homes and daily life (e.g., lotions, shampoos, cleaning supplies, soaps, and anything that goes on our skin). We can choose wisely and use more natural products. Some of these products even counter what is already inside us! And of course, the biggest thing we add to our bodies each day, that becomes our body, is food.

As an herbalist, I see that plants are powerful allies in supporting our well-being, and was taught that the many constituents of whole plants work synergistically for the best results. Now, I advocate using concentrated, pure plant essential oils for a wide variety of daily concerns along with whole food nutrition and natural solutions. Why? At this point in our history, we are exposed to concentrated toxins created by human activity—industry, chemistry, and unsustainable practices in just about every field of endeavor. We are surrounded by more highly concentrated compounds than would ever be found in nature. So, highly concentrated plant substances can help counter what we deal with now, in this day and age.

It's worth the wealth of energy, body function, brain clarity, and enhanced ability to make health practices a priority, which includes time and activity in the natural world.

Some favorite essential oil blends for health:

- Digestive Blend
- Grounding Blend
- Respiratory Blend
- Protective Blend

6: Connection to Self

When I'm dealing with drama of any sort, looking for a solution to a business tangle, struggling to find the right idea, or my mind is frazzled by too much computer work, I know getting outside will clear things up. Whether cycling, walking, swimming (when possible), or just sitting on my porch with a cat, I consider the opportunity to feel nature's spirit a priceless wealth.

It's one of the simplest tools we have to explore ourselves.

Another is journaling, which helps many of us clarify and even resolve issues. It's another easy tool to explore our inner world. The act of writing, of putting something into words seems to direct our powers of observation and insight. I remember during an herbal education class being assigned to sit with a plant of our choosing in a nature preserve area. I choose a tiny green bunch that (if I remember correctly) was pennyroyal. I didn't think I got much, but I expressed the insight received that just because something is small in size doesn't mean it's not powerful. Whoa! I guess I was taught after all. The combination of time connecting and expressing what came from it still brings me insights and ideas.

Many advisors, including happiness experts (who even knew that was a thing?), tell us that keeping a gratitude journal is one of the surest ways to progress in health, happiness, creativity, and healing. I have found that quite time outside can intensify the sense of wonder at the experience we call life.

Wordsmith Debby Kevin, by profession, helps people step fully into themselves so they can attract the people they want into their world. She uses words to do that, whether coaching a client in producing branding copy, a blog, or a book (and more).

In herself and in her clients, she's discovered the power of vulnerability, when shown from a place of healing. She came from a violently dysfunctional family, and then marriage, and told me that the natural world has been her lifeline throughout tumultuous times. For her, the sensual nature of the outdoors grounds clears, clarifies, and gets her unstuck in her work. Walking could disperse the constant on-alert cortisol her body had to produce for emergency fight or flight action. Besides draining away negative emotions, she finds her daily walks unleash creativity to better serve her clients and work of empowering women in the world.

The smell of the air or pine trees, the sound of birds, the all-encompassing experience of time at a lake, or in the mountains, hiking or camping grounds and supports her. A favorite family story is of the adults discussing who would take turns carrying the then 4-year-old Debby on a long mountain hike they had planned. They were all impressed and more than a little surprised that she walked the entire way.

Today she says that if she doesn't get at least an hour outside every day, preferably walking, she's off her game and just doesn't feel the energy or insight she must have to function well.

Debby's Wealthy in the Woods
Debby pictures a home, probably Cape Cod style that has a forest just beyond the backyard. From her window, she can see deer,

birds, and other wildlife in her yard. Maybe a fox shows up now and then. There's a creek burbling nearby which can be heard from her bedroom window, and sometimes she's awakened by the tap-tap-tap of a woodpecker. Inside there's a big stone fireplace to welcomes guests and family alike, as well as pillows to lean against and a pot of tea to share. Other times, she and her company will enjoy a glass of wine and a board game. Big French doors let in daylight and bring the outdoor beauty closer. She visualizes another stone fireplace to gather around outside. One rule regarding the possessions she allows in this home is that they each have meaning to her. This means less stuff, but more satisfaction with what is there. She cultivates a sense of peace, joy, connection in this place (and personally I want to visit her there, please!).

Essential oils Debby uses to focus on and enhance her writing are:

- Lavender to relax, calm, and release stress
- Frankincense for grounding, perspective, and protection
- Peppermint to uplift, encourage, and love herself

7: Walking for Your Life

I used to see a movie or television show (*Little House on the Prairie* comes to mind) and wondered how a farmer could work all day in the fields and then come home in the evening, pick up his fiddle, and play for fun with his family. Now I understand. While it's not my everyday lifestyle, there have been a few times when I've worked in my garden for hours, helped to build our house, or had an active day at the beach. My body had lots of physical activity, but my brain felt refreshed, creative, and ready to engage. Obviously, there's a physical exhaustion point where sleep is needed more than creative expression, but in suburban life, it doesn't happen often. It's interesting that after doing sedentary computer or other brain work, I reach a point of tiredness where I have a hard time making myself do anything physical or mental. And if I'm feeling uninspired, a walk or bike ride outside refreshes my mental capacity as well as my body.

Outdoors works better than indoors.

A fantasy I have and am heading toward making a reality is to make healthy habits integral to my job. Translation: I desire to be paid for doing physical activity; preparing food and eating wisely; getting enough rest and massage; and whatever else I need for high-level wellness.

My friend Heather Waring is already in that mode. She creates long and short walking experiences for women, to give them time and space for thought, recuperation, exploring what they truly want for their lives, and then to get it. She wants people to know that this process and experience can transform their lives.

Based near London, England, she walks out her door to green surroundings or crosses the channel to other countries. Her five-day Camino Experience walk has attracted people from both sides of the pond and transformed their lives.

Heather finds that time walking and talking (or not talking) outdoors brings us into the moment, completely present. When paying attention, it's amazing to notice something new or different along the way. Walking slows us down, taking us of out of our frenzied mind space and into a powerful calm that lasts far beyond the walk itself, hours and days even. We can "take a problem for a walk" where our focus is sharpened, and yet we let go trying for a solution at the same time. On the other hand, we can leave a problem completely behind for a while. Either way, Heather often goes home with ideas that make a difference.

Nature supports this work directly. It's a multi-faceted way to love ourselves. We get some exercise, a time-out, or a healthy escape. It's an investment to clarify what is deeply important to us and to understand better what we may need an escape from. Women, especially, tend to stay so busy caring for everyone else that we become somewhat superficial.

She says that sometimes while on a group walk a couple of women who didn't before know each other before will go deep into conversation. Perhaps one of the reasons for the easy connection is that they have to watch where they're walking. Because they don't look into each other's eyes and it feels safer. Like it's sometimes easier to have a potentially emotional conversation while driving.

Walking, in particular, is now very much a part of Heather's identity. It not only saved her life physically and emotionally from burnout and severe adrenal fatigue, it now affects her choices in other aspects of her life. Experiencing how the natural world influences her, she's more aware of environmental issues, details of nature, and the world in general. She is more thoughtful choosing what she puts into her body, what she puts on her skin, and what she wears, uses, and buys. She asks, "Where did it come from? How does it affect the world?"

Heather's Wealthy in the Woods
It looks like being supported (including being paid) to walk all the time. To easily be able to explore more places and to take people on the walking journey to find themselves, to help others feel the abundance she already feels when she's outdoors. She's walking her talk, literally!

As part of choosing wisely what she exposes her body to, this amazing woman has basil in her office, because the scent energizes and focuses her on the writing part of her business. She loves rosemary and lavender and sees the benefit of using plant-based means to deal with sore muscles and joints, with blisters and mental fatigue. Also, she loves:

- Basil for focus and energy
- Lavender for calming
- Rosemary for memory and clarity
- Soothing Blend for occasional muscle or joint stiffness

8: Energy of the Land

At this point, most of us have some access to nature if we choose it. We're part of this heritage and wealth the earth provides, even though there are wounds and pain associated with land and the life on it. I've found that simplifying the human-made part of my life allows the richness in.

Sometimes we need to experience what we don't want to figure out what we do want. For me, it's happened more than once. I'm ready to simplify because I know the emotional (and sometimes physical) heaviness of having too much. I am beginning to honor myself by refusing to spend much of my time on activities that don't bring light, fulfillment, or love into the world.

Kara Breese figured this out a long time ago. She had the classic American dream life with a large home, marriage, and a lucrative corporate job. She had friends and social life, but everything felt surface deep. She spent a lot of time in her head and felt disconnected from herself, empty, and deeply unhappy. As someone sensitive to vibrational energy, she studied and learned to discern and clear negative energy. This healing energy of people, animals, and land brought her a sense of purpose and fulfillment. She discovered that working with the land, in particular, radiated out to help people and other life forms.

"[By doing] home and land healing work, you are not only taking action to support your family's health, environment, and evolvement, you are also actively helping raise the vibration and consciousness of the Planet," Kara said.

She continued, "The process raises the frequency of an environment and is a catalyst for dynamic change. The quickening of the field clears old patterns as well as dense and stressful energy. It provides a supportive framework to create a new state of being (new thoughts, new choices, new actions and behaviors, new experiences, and new feelings). This new state of being opens the field for expansion, health, repair, regeneration, love/joy/trust, and connection.

"Ultimately the work supports the health and vitality of the microbes, soil, plants, animals, and people living on the property and brings the property to its highest potential."

Today that's how Kara feels deeply connected not only to herself but those around her.

My experience of connection was described in my first book, *Seven Secrets of Shining*. One day as I walked along a paved street lined on one side with trees, I noticed something I never had before. In my head and heart, I could FEEL a difference of energy and spirit, when I looked upon the trees as compared to the street. The trees felt of strength, depth, and life flow. The street felt blank, stuck, and blocked. I felt with clarity my need to be nourished by nature and creation.

Kara's Wealthy in the Woods
Spending time daily in direct contact with fresh air, ground, plants, water, and animals is wealth. We are incomplete without it no matter how much money or things we have. The irony is that abundant income allows us to be or go into those outdoor areas much more easily, getting away from the usual activities that bring the money. What if our income was generated by connecting with nature, self, spirit, and each other? And by connecting with self, I mean discovering, developing, and sharing our gifts, talents, and mission here on earth.

I asked Kara about her favorite essential oils, and she exclaimed: "Oh gosh! So many amazing choices!"

Essential Oils she frequently uses and what she says about them:

- Protective Blend is perfect for a little boost and sense of protection when I'm feeling run down
- Digestive Blend always comes to the rescue to help soothe tummy discomfort. It's the perfect travel companion.
- Encouraging Blend is incredible for meditation and connecting with Spirit. The connection is immediate.
- Peppermint is one essential oil she loves to use after brushing her teeth to further support mouth health.
- Inspiring Blend is used to increase creativity.
- Cedarwood is great for grounding and coming back to Earth following Spiritual work or for simply kicking off the day.

Her current favorite is created by mixing the Inspiring Blend with Cedarwood. She finds the combination intoxicating.

9: Animals: Our Companions

We humans seem to have a driving hunger to connect with animals, especially when we barely get to be outdoors. True, our fur babies aren't exactly part of the wilderness, but their companionship and unconditional love help us cope with modern stresses.

Just a few days ago, our local newspaper reported that when it comes to taking care of pets, a third of U.S. owners claim money is no object. Some studies show that petting a cat daily can lower blood pressure and that more than half of pet dogs sleep with their people. A friend of mine does entire retreats for people based on interactions and the intuition of her horses.

We long to connect even more directly with the animals in our lives. Maribeth Decker, an animal communicator who lives in Virginia, works remotely with people from all over the world. She helps them figure out what their pets are trying to say to them. She describes her ability to commune with an animal's thoughts and feelings like tuning into a radio station. People especially want to understand their animals when the animals are stressed, anxious, morose, or in pain. Maribeth often finds that animals want to find their place in the family. She especially supports the family when either the animal or its' human is ready to pass away. Ready to transition, as Maribeth would say.

Maribeth came to animal communication by way of seeking to connect with nature. A far cry from her previous career in the military, she couldn't deny that her softer, empathetic side was calling to be developed. She became a Reiki master, participated

Quantum Touch, energy healing, and shamanic studies, all of which led her to recognize the inherent power and connection we all have with the natural world.

Maribeth's not usually the first person someone seeks out when they sense something is off with their animal. Often, the animal has been trundled off to veterinarians, trainers, other traditional professionals, without noticeable results. Pet guardians are often initially skeptical, which disappears as soon as they witness the effectiveness of Maribeth's work.

Why does she offer her ability and service in animal communication? She has a big WHY and a smaller WHY. The big WHY is a desire to be part of the movement bringing understanding and respect between species. It is sacred, life-affirming work, and bigger than any one person. The smaller, personal WHY involves bringing animal communication into hospitals and homes to relieve the pain and suffering of others. It's also obvious to me as I get to know Maribeth that she get a great deal of enjoyment and satisfaction from this work. She loves her clients, both furry and human.

Wealthy in the Woods for Maribeth
After her first thought of making sure she lived near water, a river, or stream, she said, "Let's have some fun with this!" If she knew her five animals were taken care of, she would frequently travel to visit great natural areas of the world, places like Yellowstone, Africa, and Alaska. Ideally, she'd like to skip the travel time and "beam" over to various locations for the weekend (me, too!). Or, given current technology, maybe take a train or have someone else take care of the travel logistics.

My favorite Maribeth quote, "I like being a suburbanite, but also need the raw stuff." Amen.

Currently, she uses the following essential oils:

- Lavender on a neckerchief for her dog that gets anxious with the sound of sirens
- Oregano diluted in Fractionated Coconut Oil (FCO) for skin issues on her smaller dog
- Respiratory Blend diffused during the winter months
- Restful Blend and Reassuring Blend diffused to help a new kitten relax
- Tension Blend to relieve her stress
- Protective Blend Cleaner because animals, like people, absorb easily through the bottom of their feet, and she wants safe substances on the floor

She's also exploring the use of essential oils for emotional management for animals as well as for people. She finds humans are the emotional leaders in a household or family, so where they affect their pets.

10: Love Our Convenience!

Why did I choose to ally with particular companies?

Wealthy in the woods is the juxtaposition of who I am. I grew up in the United States suburbs, an active childhood that included boating, water sports, making forts, acting out stories, bicycling, playing along with a whole lot of reading, some music, and organized sports, gymnastics mostly.

I studied western health care, earning a bachelor's degree in nursing. Later, I studied herbal medicine, because I wanted to understand how to use plants for health purposes. I called it a preparedness interest, getting me ready to take care of myself and the people I cared about if pharmaceutical medicines weren't available.

I found much more than expected. I discovered a whole different way of living and looking at the world, which included food, body care, home items, gardening, foraging or wildcrafting, and acknowledging the spirit of the natural world. A way of honoring and living much more in sync with natural patterns. This knowledge dovetailed beautifully with my inclinations toward communing with outdoor life. Don't get me wrong! I still appreciate technology, safety from bodily harm, shelter from the elements, and modern comforts.

I don't believe they are mutually exclusive. The chance to travel to Greece, Italy, Britain, and other countries has shown me how much the North American culture gears toward convenience.

I often remember a line from Don Aslett, author of books about designing and taking care of a home, "the greatest predictor of behavior is convenience." I've since observed this truth. For instance, Aslett suggests that the best way to plan a walking path on a piece of property is to watch where people tend to walk. If the grass is planted on the most convenient route, there would be a constant battle to keep people off the grass. Kinda funny, but doesn't it feel true?

So we like our convenience, and that means the products I use and endorse are convenient.

I insist on a positive, aware, uplifting company culture if I'm going to be involved. I want to see a track record of integrity, sound principles, and leaders with skin in the game. I expect this along with the potential for significant income, even residual income. I see that in both my chosen Essential Oils Company* and SendOutCards.

Essential oils are aromatic plant components in small, easily used, and stored bottles that can support our desire to use natural products, since most of us won't grow, harvest, dry, process, and prepare our own plant tonics. Personally, I love picking herbs fresh from my backyard for tea, poultices, or cooking. I still use oils both indoors and out.

SendOutCards fits me because, like most small business owners, I want to treat my customers well. I am more likely to send a physical card, with the occasional gift when it's easy, convenient, and affordable. If I can upload a photo from my phone and write a personal message using an online service that then prints the card, stuffs it into an envelope, addresses it, stamps it, and mails it for us, I'm in. I enjoy celebrating people's life events and accomplishments, the seasonal changes and holidays, and developing friendships with a diverse network of good people.

Being a child of natural and modern worlds, I believe we can be a bridge uniting them to bring the best of both worlds together. The internet allows worldwide association and projects. Travel is more accessible than ever, and there are ways to afford pretty much whatever we want. Heck, we can even be wealthy in the woods!

*The oil company I collaborate with is consistently determined to stay within legal and regulatory boundaries, and this book is not published by them, so they prefer I don't use their name. I'm proud of our association and will gladly chat with you about essential oils over the phone or via email. Contact me at nwherbalist@comcast.net to set up a time to talk.

11: The Network Marketing Tool

What's the nitty-gritty of Wealth in the Woods? To me, it has a steady income that easily supports my chosen lifestyle, causes, and purposes. One that includes beauty (both natural and created by people), health, family, travel, learning, and humanitarian causes, fulfilling my life mission, and more.

I believe economic income is true empowerment. Not money in and of itself, but what we can do with it. Money has neutral energy that will become active once we use it.

Money is a magnifier. A good person will magnify the good they do if they have more money. It allows time and financial freedom, talent development, and health restoration. It can be used to relieve suffering, invite calm, and make happy memories. Obviously, it could be used for harm as well, magnifying the intentions of whoever controls it. But for most of us, having money creates the freedom to contribute and live our highest purposes as well as our dreams.

What's so wonderful is that we attract prosperity BECAUSE we share our message, light, and who we are or decide to be. It attracts the people, opportunities, and resources to fulfill our highest causes.

The greatest freedom happens with leveraged or residual income. Residual income meaning a paycheck related to past work that continues after the work is done. Residual income can come from royalties like authors and artists receive, from investment income, rental income, or from leveraging your expertise. For simplicity and having a home base, it's hard to beat a network marketing prime or add-on business.

If you own a heart-centered business that matches well with a network marketing company's products, you can use both to serve your clients and develop a network of others who do the same. This model magnifies your influence for good as well as creates a substantial income stream.

It's sometimes called direct marketing, relationship marketing, or multi-level marketing, but the term "network marketing" is the most accurate, IMO.

How Network Marketing meets the freedom criteria
I've spent the last five years observing, studying, and learning from very successful network marketing professionals in a variety of companies. These are seven-figure earners who are happy to share their skills, tools, and mindset for the benefit of others. It's a common trait of successful people in this profession. They repeatedly remind us that a network or direct marketing business:

- Offers true equal opportunity. Often, it highlights the face and power of women;
- Has unlimited potential with no income cap;
- Can be done alongside whatever else you do, so it offers flexible work time;
- Is recommended by such business powerhouses as Robert Kiyosaki and Richard Branson; and
- Multiplies your efforts as you help others duplicate simple actions.

I have a nice sized group of several dedicated leaders who are growing their businesses and taking good care of their teams. I am grateful for them and love to support and celebrate them as they continue their progress. It took a couple intense spurts of work to develop this group, but I now have a truly residual income that comes with very little effort. My fun and joy are helping others also get to that point, whatever their income goals are.

Because I know my life work to be connecting us with nature, self, spirit, and each other, I choose to ally myself with the two companies mentioned earlier, for plant essential oils and SendOutCards for keeping in touch in convenient and personalized ways.

You want stats? I got stats!

- Network Marketing is over a hundred years old, and a twenty-eight billion dollar industry in the U.S. (as of 2009 research by the Direct Selling Association).
- Worldwide, it is approximately a $114 billion profession involving about sixty-five million people. Comparisons from Kody Bateman, founder of SendOutCards, show that the NFL is a nine billion dollar industry, worldwide music industry sixty-six point four billion dollars, and movies and entertainment worldwide are $109.4 billion industries.
- Sixty-seven percent of buying decisions are driven by word of mouth, and ninety percent of customers say word of mouth is the most reliable, trustworthy source of product information. Compare this to fourteen percent for advertisers and eight percent for celebrities. (Global research and consultant company McKenzie)

Our Auto-pilot Objections
While some people have experienced the potential and opportunity network marketing provides, there are others who have negative, limiting beliefs about it. They think things like:

- It has to be excruciatingly hard to learn and hard to do
- To be successful, I will be deprived of all my currently enjoyable activities
- Talking to other people about this will bother people, and I could lose friends
- The products cost too much
- I don't have time

- I'm not a salesperson
- I don't know anyone
  I'm too old/young/large/small/have no experience;
- It's a pyramid scheme
- I've seen people have bad experiences or lose money with Network Marketing

I've felt most of these and have searched to develop the attitudes and practices that make them false in my life. I sought and found simplicity, sought and found ways to make time alongside everything else in my life. I sought and found ways that living my work can enhance and deepen relationships rather than damage them. I am SO not a salesperson, and that can work to advantage since others sense the quiet strength of knowing rather than slick attempts to convince. And on and on.

Jordan Adler, a million dollar plus network marketing professional, has a book called *Beach Money* that inspires us with reasonable, yet amazing principles to help us reach our envisioned income. How'd you like to make *Beach Money*, as in making money while relaxing at the beach?

Last but not least, these kinds of income streams and businesses can be developed anywhere we can get an internet connection- which means in the woods works just fine.

Essential oils for focus, energy, motivation, and manifesting:

- Massage Blend to relax tense muscles
- Focus Blend when I need extra attention to a project
- Lemongrass to help clear negative emotions
- Encouraging Blend for energizing and encouraging
- Inspiring Blend to be aware of big WHYs and passions
- Detoxification Blend for vitality and transition

12: Exploring Further

Through my business, ASPEN Living, LLC (aspenliving.org), I take the stand that connection with nature is vital to our health and happiness and the world. It impacts our physical, mental, emotional, and spiritual aspects as well as relationships. I use plant essential oils and proven keep-in-touch tools to collaborate with like-minded people worldwide (especially entrepreneurs) to facilitate and support those connections.

I believe that combining my gifts with the strengths, energy, passion, and unique brilliance of people who share similar values can lift all of us and influence the world for good.

You have expertise and resources I don't, and maybe I have some that can bless, build, heal, and inspire you.

Would you like to explore the possibilities? If you feel an attraction, it may be that we have potential synergy and can build on that.

I'd love to hear about your work and passion and what you would like to see more of in your business or career. If I can't help, I may know someone who can and am glad to refer you.

Set up a get-acquainted call by texting me at 503.334.9114.

May your version of Wealthy in the Woods be your reality soon!

Note: for more information about essential oils, I usually set up an appointment. We discuss your health needs and concerns, a little bit about the company I use, and our most popular kits. My part of the call takes about thirty minutes. You're under no obligation to purchase, but should you choose to do so, I can help you.

Recommended Books

- *The 4 Laws of Financial Prosperity* by Blaine Harris and Charles Coonradt
- *12 Steps to Whole Foods* by Robyn Openshaw
- *Beach Money* by Jordan Adler
- *The Big Leap* by Gay Hendricks
- *The China Study* by T. Colin Campbell
- *Dressing Your Truth* by Carol Tuttle
- *Embrace Your Magnificence* by Fabienne Fredrickson
- *The Go-Giver* by Bob Burg and John David Mann
- *Go Pro* by Eric Worre
- *The Healing Earth* by Philip Sutton Chard
- *Heal Your Body A-Z* by Louise Hay
- *Last Child in the Woods* by Richard Louv
- *The Life-Changing Magic of Tidying Up* by Marie Kondo
- *Making the First Circle Work* by Randy Gage
- *Referral of a Lifetime* by Tim Templeton
- *Sharing and Caring* by Ilene Meckley
- *The Slight Edge* by Jeff Olson
- *SpOil Your Pet* by Mia K. Frezzo, D.V.M.
- *Strength Finder 2.0* by Tom Rath
- *David's Pure Vegetarian Kitchen* by David A. Gabbe
- *Your Money or Your Life* by Vicki Robin and Joe Dominguez

Essential Oils Reference

Basil helps keep skin looking clean, bright, and healthy. Promotes mental alertness and lessons anxious feelings. Supports cardiovascular and nervous system health.

Cedarwood repels insects, promotes relaxation, and helps keep skin looking healthy.

Detoxification Blend supports healthy liver function and body's natural ability to rid itself of unwanted substances, purifying and detoxifying the body's systems. Contains tangerine peel, rosemary leaf, geranium flower/leaf, juniper berry, and cilantro herb essential oils.

Digestive Blend supports healthy digestion; soothes occasional stomach upset, bloating, gas, and indigestion. Contains anise seed, peppermint plant, ginger root, caraway seed, coriander seed, tarragon plant, and fennel seed essential oils.

Encouraging Blend promotes feelings of confidence, courage, and belief; counteracts emotions of doubt, pessimism, and cynicism. Contains peppermint plant, clementine peel, coriander seed, basil herb, yuzu peel, Melissa leaf/flower, rosemary leaf essential oils, and vanilla bean absolute.

Focus Blend, a study-time blend, enhances and sustains a sense of focus, supports efforts of those who have difficulty paying attention and staying on task. Contains Amyris bark, patchouli leaf, frankincense resin, lime peel, ylang-ylang flower, Hawaiian sandalwood wood, and Roman chamomile flower essential oils.

Grounding Blend was explicitly designed for emotional grounding. It promotes a whole-body sense of relaxation; helps evoke feelings of tranquility and balance, and may help ease anxious feelings. Contains fractionated coconut oil along with spruce leaf, ho wood leaf, frankincense resin, blue tansy flower, blue chamomile flower, and Osmanthus flower essential oils.

Inspiring Blend ignites feelings of excitement, passion, and joy; counteracts feelings of boredom and disinterest. Contains fractionated coconut oil along with cardamom seed, cinnamon bark, ginger rhizome, clove bud. Sandalwood wood essential oils, jasmine flower absolute, vanilla bean absolute, and damiana leaf essential oil.

Lavender soothes occasional skin irritations, helps reduce anxious feelings and promotes peaceful sleep, and has a relaxing aroma.

Lemongrass is a powerful cleanser of energy. Refreshing, supports healthy digestion, soothing massage oil (when diluted in a carrier oil).

Massage Blend is comforting, relaxing, helps to lessen tension. Contains cypress leaf, peppermint plant, marjoram leaf, basil leaf, grapefruit peel, and lavender flower essential oils.

Oregano is a powerful cleansing and purifying agent for both the body and other surfaces. It's important to dilute in carrier oil when used on the skin as it can be irritating to sensitive areas. Emotionally, it is the oil of humility and as well as non-attachment.

Peppermint promotes healthy respiratory function and clear breathing, relaxing yet refreshing to mental state and alertness, relieving occasional digestive upset, and naturally repels bugs.

Protective Blend supports healthy immune and respiratory function, the body's natural antioxidant defenses, with an energizing and uplifting aroma. It is also a powerful surface cleaner. Contains wild orange peel, clove bud, cinnamon leaf, cinnamon bark, eucalyptus leaf, rosemary leaf essential oils.

Reassuring Blend is the oil blend of emotional peace. Contains vetiver root, lavender, ylang-ylang flower, frankincense, clary sage, marjoram leaf oil, labdanum leaf/stem extract, and spearmint oil.

Respiratory Blend supports the respiratory system, promotes feelings of clear airways, and a restful night's sleep. Contains laurel leaf, eucalyptus leaf, peppermint plant, melaleuca leaf, lemon peel, ravensara leaf, and cardamom seed essential oils.

Restful Blend is the oil of tranquility. It helps calm stressed-out and overwhelmed feelings. Contains lavender, cedarwood, Hopwood leaf, ylang-ylang flower, marjoram leaf, Roman chamomile flower, vetiver root oils, vanilla bean extract, and Hawaiian sandalwood oil.

Rosemary supports healthy digestion and respiratory functions and helps to reduce nervous tension and occasional fatigue.

Soothing Blend is soothing and cooling applied externally. Contains wintergreen leaf, camphor bark, peppermint plant, ylang-ylang flower, helichrysum flower, blue tansy flower, blue chamomile flower, and Osmanthus flower essential oils.

Tension Blend is the oil of releasing and relief, both physically and emotionally. Contains wintergreen, lavender, peppermint, frankincense, cilantro, marjoram, Roman chamomile, basil, and rosemary.

Index and Resources

Chapter 5

- https://www.dietsinreview.com/diet_column/06/a-carrot-had-more-nutrients-50-years-ago-than-it-does-today/
- https://www.scientificamerican.com/article/soil-depletion-and-nutrition-loss/

Chapter 6

Contact Deborah Kevin at https://deborahkevin.com

Chapter 7

Contact Heather Waring at https://womenwalkingwomentalking.com

Chapter 8

Contact Kara Breese at https://karabreese.com

Chapter 9

Contact Maribeth Decker at https://sacredgrove.com

Acknowledgments

I love the principles and practices taught by such business greats as Bob Burg in *Go-Giver*, Tim Templeton in *The Referral of a Lifetime*, Eric Worre in *Go Pro*, and Michael J. Cohen in *Reconnecting with Nature*. In them, I see the natural, true, authentic, trustworthy, spiritual, and loving business person I always seek to be and have learned ways to run my business with those values.

Talk about not going it alone! Participating in Boldheart Business, created by Fabienne Fredrickson, with her larger-than-life presence and light, gave the vision and deadlines to create this book. Each of the people I've met through this organization has contributed to their acceptance, vision, energy, and caring. Okay, I have to name some names (alphabetically)— Maribeth Decker, Lira Kanaan, Debby Kevin, Kiva Schuler, Heather Waring, and more all the time.

I appreciate the head, heart, and soul given by my network marketing group leaders. In the essential oil company that includes Natalie Goddard, Laura Jacobs, and Marlyn Diderickson. In SendOutCards, it's Jordan Adler, Mark Herdering, and Kellie Grill. They believe in me even as they forgive my failings and teach me with every interaction.

Finally, I am continually grateful for unquestioning support from my husband, Tom, and the tolerance of my family as I grow in many directions. I am blessed and wish that for each reader as well.

About the Author

Debbie Tuttle is a big-picture kind of gal who loves sharing how life-enriching principles and practices fit together into a holistic wellness lifestyle. Her degree in nursing, the study of herbalism, experience as a wellness and fitness educator, spiritual practices, and personal journey allow her to recognize high-quality opportunities for creating greater light. Her passions include seeing people's superpowers, pointing them out, supporting and celebrating their development and successes.

She lives in the beautiful Pacific Northwest U.S. with her husband, Tom, and various children/ grandchildren/ cats, depending on the year. She enjoys local, and national travel for business and especially loves visiting her four grown, married children and her totally wonderful grandchildren. She gets into cycling, yoga, tai-chi, Hawaii, green smoothies, many genres of music, and sharing resources that connect people to nature and each other, to name a few.

She uses network marketing culture and products in her A.S.P.E.N. Living business to unite, bless, and build as many people as possible. Contact her at nwherbalist@comcast.net.

www.ingramcontent.com/pod-product-compliance
Lightning Source LLC
Chambersburg PA
CBHW070948220526
45471CB00007B/2947